Died at Birth

A child's life of heartache & growth

Toya Heywood-Grinnage

Died at Birth

Copyright © 2017 by Toya Heywood-Grinnage

ISBN: 978-0-9970918-4-7

All rights reserved. Printed in the United States of America. Except as permitted under the United States Copyright Act of 1976, no part of this book may be reproduced or transmitted in any form or by any means without written permission of the author.

A product of: Destiny Publishings LLC.
Editor: Phelice Stevenson
Cover Model: Madison Carter Bolaji
Cover Design: Oluwaseyi Bolaji
          BLUEDISK LLC.

Acknowledgments

I want to thank my family for pushing me to strive for the best. I thank God for blessing me with children that not only look up to me, but I can look to them as well. My beautiful princess D'Amani. You have blessed me with your wisdom, intelligence and encouraging words when I needed them most. Neveah, my baby girl, thank you for having patience with me. I also thank you for teaching and showing me how love felt again with your many hugs and kisses. To my loving son, David, who was there with me through it all. Thank you for keeping a smile on my face with your love, jokes and that amazing personality that you share with me and others. I want to thank God for creating a husband just for me. Thank you, Hun, for being you. Thank you for overshadowing me with your love and treating me like the jewel that I am. Thank you for not abusing the blessing that God has given you. From the day we met you've been a blessing, and I'm honored to call you my husband.

Table of Contents

Mental Rollercoaster 1

The Unwanted Relative **5**

Turning Point 11

New Beginnings 19

Letting Go **27**

God's Grace 39

Still Standing 51

Words of Encouragement... 65

Introduction

I was not able to fully take it in as I stood there in complete awe, not believing this day had finally come. I was finally marrying the one just for me—a friend, provider, a man, a lover, and father to my children. So, there I stood, holding my breath, waiting to be awakened from a dream. With that same breath, I asked myself if I could do this despite everything that I have endured in life.

It's sad when you've been through so much that you've forgotten how love and happiness feels. Five months had gone and my inner man still wrestled with the fact that it was okay to smile and to be pampered. It also helped knowing that I had God, my husband and my children to remind me that it was okay. They continuously give me strength to move forward despite my past.

For years, I'd pondered if I would ever be that girl who would get married. Would I ever find love and be happy? So many things had happened in my life that I'd gotten to the point where I had started saying, "It is what it is?" I believed that if it was supposed to happen, then it would happen. If not, then oh well—it won't. I'd gotten used to the pain. Loneliness had become second nature to me and misery was a part of my being.

Let's go back to the beginning. My life was not peaches and cream. Maybe the peaches, but no cream. From the time, I was in my mother's womb, God had a plan for me that the devil did not want fulfilled. Back in September of 1978, a child was born. But before the birth—before the moment my mother could hold her baby—there was a death that took place. While in my mother's womb, I died. My heart stopped pumping the necessary blood needed to survive. I was deprived of oxygen.

The doctors rushed my mother to the operating room for an emergency C-section. They kicked my father out of the room and sent him to the waiting area. Dad waited there frantically, not knowing what would happen. My mother laid there praying to God, "Please don't let me come this far and you take my baby. Please bring her back to me". Needless to say, I'm here. Glory to God! In that short precious moment of life, I encountered my first, but not last, experience with death.

"Before I formed you in the womb I knew you, before you were born I set you apart; I appointed you as a prophet to the nations" Jeremiah 1:5-6.

Mental Rollercoaster

Growing up as I remember, life was pretty-good. Things looked great to me. We had our ups and downs. There were more downs than ups but hey, there's no perfect family, right? I had most of the things I wanted, but not always what I needed. Things seemed to look good in my eyes, as related to my family. That is, until the day reality set in and I was old enough to realize what was really, going on.

I was about 8 or 9-years old when I started realizing something was not quite right. There was a lot of arguing and fighting that led to hurt and pain in my house. One day, I remember hearing my parents fighting. It was very intense for a young girl of my age, or for any child to hear.

Died at Birth

One day my parents were in an altercation in their bedroom. When it seemed to be over, I decided to go in and check on my mom. I saw her laying down on the bed with tears resting on her face. There was a huge knot on her head. Rubbing my mother's back and wiping her tears away I said, "It's going to be okay". At the same time, I was glaring at my dad with looks that could kill. I remember that day like it was yesterday. That was the moment I started losing respect for him. Even though I was always known as daddy's little girl, I was crushed, because I saw a side of him that I wish I'd never seen.

As time passed, things died down with mom and dad. Now there was conflict with one of my siblings and my parent. Their clashes stemmed from the household pain. By this time arguing and fighting became normal behavior at my house and I was used to it. I tried to convince myself that this is how families interact, this is what family is all about -

even though deep down inside - I did not believe it. All around me, I saw families arguing and fighting, especially in my neighborhood. Not too many people showed love.

They interpreted love as buying the child what they wanted. "So, what the heck! I guess this is the way it is", I thought to myself. I never understood how a family who said we loved each other, hurt each other. How can you say you "love," but with the same energy, you raise your hand to strike? It had to be more to life than this.

I began to lose all sense of hope. My hope of having a perfect family died. My thoughts of mom and dad living a good life together died. My identity started to change. I started to feel like things were happening because of me. I was emotionally and mentally gone.

"Yea, though I walk through the valley of the shadow of death, I will fear no evil: for thou art with me; thy rod and thy staff they comfort me" (Psalm 23:4).

The Unwanted Relative

Who would have thought that this unwanted relative would come to visit our home? Have you ever had a friend or family member ask if they could stay at your house until they get on their feet? Maybe a month, they say? Of course, you say yes. Then, however, that month goes to six months, then to a year…or more.

That's what happened to us—except our unwanted relative came to kill, steal and to destroy our home, my peace and my mind. At the time this unwanted relative came, I was clueless of the plans this unwanted relative had for my family. I knew something was a little different with mom though, but unaware that the damage had already started. With my natural eye, things still looked pretty, good. We still had clothes on our backs, food on the table, fun times at the park, we went to amusement parks, and enjoyed some other niceties of life. Why would I have thought anything different?

Since I'm exposing this relative, I might as well give you his name. "CRACK COCAINE". Yeah, that's it, CRACK.

This drug, this big black demon, this stronghold, this disgrace to society, "Why are you here?" I screamed. "Why have you come? Who invited you? Who opened the door to let you in? What do you want?" I mean, I saw it on television. I even saw it outside on the street. But "never", I said, "in my house". It was hard to believe. How did my home become affected and infected by this ugly demon?

As time went on, I saw less of my dad and siblings. It was just me, mom, and crack in my house. It came in and gradually took over my mother's mind. The loneliness caused me to emotionally with draw. I started spending more time with my cabbage patch dolls to fill the void. They were the only ones I could talk to and the only ones who listened to me. They saw my tears. All the peace, happiness, and confidence that I once had, started to die. No longer did I care. This precious little girl who had so much love in her heart started to wither away. This unwanted family member invited itself into my house. It manipulated my mother's mind, made her feel whole, consoled her inner pain, and told her that it loved her. As she wrestled back and forth, it told her, *"Don't kick me out. I can help you. I can protect you"*.

After a while, I realized this thing was not going anywhere, so instead of spending my time with my dolls, I started spending the night with friends and at my relatives' houses. One night I slept over at a friend's house. I was about 11-years- old. After playing, we'd all fallen asleep. I ended up on the couch. While sleeping, I kept feeling something but I wasn't sure what it was. I felt it again, woke up, looked around, and didn't see anything. So, I went back to sleep thinking I was dreaming. I experienced this feeling for about three more times, until the last time, I woke up and saw a man standing over me; touching me. I quickly screamed and got up and ran to the back of the house and told my friend's mother.

I learned that the man who was standing over me was my friend's uncle. I felt so violated at that moment—not only violated, but ashamed. I was so upset with my mom because I felt like if things were different at home, this would not have happened. I carried so much pain to the point where I became a rebellious child. I was so angry at life, my mom and at God. "Why is this happening to me? What did I do to deserve this?", I said to myself. This 11-year-old girl no longer understood why she was here or why God created her. What was the point of her being born? Only time will tell.

The Unwanted Relative

"I have given you authority to trample on snakes and scorpions and to overcome all the power of the enemy; nothing will harm you", Luke 10:19.

Turning Point

As I mentioned in the previous chapter, I became rebellious and started looking for something to fill the emptiness inside. I started dating this boy, not knowing at the time this was going to be another disaster in my life. My parents knew nothing about the relationship I was in. Things in the relationship looked good in the beginning, especially to a young girl looking for attention and love. After a few years of dating, things started to unfold in my life—or should I say, unravel?

I died to my own soul and opened myself up to a boy and allowed him to enter in. The spirits he carried also entered. From my perspective, it looked so innocent. I thought I was grown and that I knew what I was doing. Little did I know, I was digging a bigger grave for myself. As young ladies. we may think we know what's best for us. Things looked so good to the eye. I did not realize that the devil was painting a picture to make things look good but things were far from good. This way of thinking is all in our imagination. It fools us into hoping and wishing that the relationship is the best thing that's ever happened to us. That part of our brain that goes into deep thoughts and imagine that perfect life with our soulmate, that's the image the devil always makes look so good. It is the same image that comes to destroy us.

A few months down the line, my mother found out about the relationship and she was extremely upset. To make it very plain, she was pissed off. Everybody knew this boy wasn't the greatest. The only reason my mom found out about him is because I got pregnant. I felt ashamed and embarrassed. I knew that I was better than that. At the same time, I didn't care what people thought about me. Needless to say, I had an abortion. It was a horrible experience but in my mind, it had to be done.

Turning Point

A few years into the relationship, things started getting crazy. I was now in high school. I started to experience this thing called physical abuse. I saw little signs before the abuse began to happen, but I ignored them. A little piece of wisdom: 1) When a boy/man has a crazy temper and is disrespectful to others; that's your first sign. As females, we must be careful. We get so caught up in our feelings and become fascinated with the attention we get from that boy/man so much, that we ignore the signs that are right in front of our faces. The yelling and controlling behavior are all signs to run before you get too deep. This is not only in a physically abusive relationship but any relationship--no matter what type of abuse it is. A little piece of advice: 2) Ladies or gentlemen, if you meet someone who has several different babies' mothers or babies' daddies, or you know that the male/female is very promiscuous, I advise you again, to leave that person alone. Please.

Died at Birth

What makes you think he/she is going to be faithful to you?

There are times when we may not know the hidden secrets about a person's life. However, there is always some type of sign that we tend to ignore. With me, I've seen all the signs, but I continued in relationships that were damaging to me. The funny thing about my first relationship was that the physical abuse didn't start until my father moved out of state. My fourth year into the relationship, he felt like he had power over me. I remember my first encounter with him hitting me. I didn't know if I wanted to tell my parents or keep it to myself, because I thought I loved him. My biggest mistake was keeping it a secret.

I kept my issues away from my parents, knowing if my dad found out it would not have been good. Besides, I thought that was love and it was normal to go through this in relationships. I said to myself, "What is the point of telling my dad, when, excuse me but, HELL! He, was beating on someone else's daughter". I never understood how a man can get upset when he hears that his mother, daughter, sister, was being beaten by their boyfriend or husband when, they too may have hit another man's daughter, mother or sister. I never understood that. If you don't want anyone hitting on your family member, what makes you think it's okay to do the same to someone else.

I remember this one night particularly out of all the fights we had. I was with friends enjoying myself. I'd come back home and as I walked back into the complex, I bumped into this dude and he was mad. So, what do you think happened that night? We started fighting in the street. I remember how the punk hit me so hard in my face, my lip started to swell and bleed. The crazy thing is that no one tried to stop him. People kept walking like it was the normal thing to do. After the whole ordeal was over, he realized what he had done to my face. I could tell he was scared because of his demeanor. I believe he was scared for me to go home like that, so he wanted to get a room that night. I felt like a worthless, cheap whore. I felt like dying as he sat there laughing at me. I wanted to kill him. Once we got to the room, I went to the bathroom and looked at my face and started to think back to the day when I saw my mother's face. I asked myself, as the tears began to roll down my face, *"How did I get here?"*

Later that night, he did what most men do—apologize. The crazy thing was, I fell for it. As I laid there, tears started to roll down my face. I started asking myself if this was all I was worth? The next day I went home and my mother saw the aftermath. She looked at my face and she started to cry. She called my dad and to make a long story short, that was the last time I remember him putting his hands on me.

Turning Point

A year had gone by and I was in my last year of high school. I was doing well until I got pregnant...again. I was a little disappointed but I did not let that stop me. I continued to focus on school and did what was best for me and my unborn child. With the help of my mother and a great teacher who pushed me to continue, I finished school. It was a little rough but I did not miss a beat with school other than going to doctor's appointments. I had my son on May 18th and graduated on June 6th. But before the birth of my son and before graduation, I had a dream that was so profound and it encouraged me so much.

My older brother passed away when I was about 10-years-old. He was the type of brother you could look up to, sweet hearted, laid back attitude, and just a nice person. He passed away from sickle cell. In the dream, I was walking into a church with a white cap and gown on and I sat down. I noticed in front of the sanctuary there was a casket. As I sat there staring at this casket, it started to open. It was my brother smiling at me saying, "Good job." At that point, I woke up and I knew I had to finish school. If I didn't do it for myself, I had to do it for him. That's what pushed me to do what I needed to do.

Another good thing happened. After months of praying and asking God to get me out of this relationship, he did just that! My boyfriend got locked up and went to jail. The day he went in, I started to weep; saddened by the fact that he wouldn't be around. On the other hand, I was jumping for joy that I was no longer in the mess I was in. After years of praying and wanting to get out of the relationship, I never knew it was going to be like this.

New Beginnings

I learned how to be a mom and how to live again. Believe me, it was not easy. Being a mother, on top of wanting to hang with friends was a battle because it was not about me anymore, but about my son as well. I remember one day, sitting on my bed crying and talking to my mother. I told her that I still felt trapped, like I was in a relationship; but now, with his child.

Some females get themselves into a situation like this or maybe something else, and the enemy makes them think that their life is over. You see how the devil works? When you are in a bad situation, the enemy will talk in your ear and say things like, "Stay. He loves you. Everything is just fine." But when something happens, he turns right around and makes you feel bad about yourself. Doesn't that sound like some of our so-called friends? They encourage us to stay in bad relationships but when something happens, they are talking about us behind our backs. The enemy uses anybody.

The devil will always paint a picture in your mind that you will not make it. But I'm here to tell you, life has not ended—but just begun. You can still go to school and have a great career. You can become anything you want. It's all up to you and how bad you want it. Yes, I had many more pit-falls that I put myself in, but I didn't stay there. I took each mistake as a lesson learned. Young or old, we make some crazy decisions in our lives, thinking we know what we are doing. It all can be worked out if you put in the work and are around the right people.

My son was about 3-years-old when I decided to move. I wanted something different in life. I moved to North Carolina with my dad. I lived with him for a while, got a job, then moved into my first apartment. Things were looking pretty, good for a moment, but I was still holding on to the deep pain I kept bottled up inside. As I got used to my surroundings and met new people, I started to enjoy my life.

It was about a year later when I got into a new relationship. My household grew four years later when I had another baby, a little girl. Before she was born, I went through a lot of mess with him as well. I dealt with him lying and a lot of cheating. My emotions were all over the place with this guy. We didn't get into physical altercations, instead I experienced a different type of abuse—mental and emotional. When you've been through things for so long, your body tends to get numb to everything around you. You would think after the whole ordeal of what I went through in New York, that I wouldn't take anything from anyone else. But nope! That wasn't the case for me. Instead of leaving him, I stayed. After a few more years in the relationship, I got pregnant and had my baby girl. We ended up parting ways when things did not work out.

By this time, I'd gotten to the point where I was sick and tired of being sick and tired. I knew if I wanted change, I had to do something different. I was working at the Hampton Inn and there was a church that came every Sunday to have service. One day, I decided to visit. I enjoyed it but was not fully committed. I never became a member; I would just visit from time to time. After a while, I went back to my old ways. I started hanging out with old friends and partying again.

My son was about seven years old and my daughter was around four months. I had two jobs—the hotel and a gas station. Deep down inside, I still felt like there was more to life than just this. While working there, I met this man and he was from New York as well. He was a hustler, party type guy and a drinker. But besides his downfalls, he was different from the rest of the guys. Every time he came in the store, we would look at each other, but nothing more than that. Until one day, when he wasn't with his friend, he asked me for my number. I gave him my number, but I took my time getting to know him. I wasn't so quick to get into anything because I'd just gotten out of a relationship.

About three months went by and I decided to give him a chance. We would go out from time to time. Things were going well. My dad met him and they also connected. He was always there when I needed him. The only problem I had with him was that he was a drinker. I could deal with everything else. I grew up with addiction all around me and I refused to deal with it again. We got into a lot of arguments because of it too. See, I learned in relationships that you cannot change anybody. They must want to change. In relationships, ladies think that we can change a man. NOT GOING TO HAPPEN! All we can do as women is to continue to pray for them and let God work on them. One thing I know how to do is pray.

In this relationship, he showed me so much. Even though he had his personal issues, he still knew how to be a man and take care of his jewel. He showed me love in a totally different way. I'd never felt this type of love before. Yes, I know my parents love me, but this was different; especially coming from somebody I just met. My family loved him, my children loved him and I couldn't ask for anything more.

One year, I believe it was going on 2005, I wanted to do something different for the New Year. I wanted to go to church before going out with friends. An old friend of mine and I went to this church in the area. I was sitting in the back of the church and my stomach just felt weird. I felt like the preacher was going to call on me. Lo and behold, he did. He spoke into my life and gave some me encouraging words from God. Later that night, I felt so different. Let's just say that visit at church messed up my high, LOL. I didn't know at the time God was already doing something in me.

After a few months went by, I decided to go back to that church for a visit. A couple of months later, I joined. I started growing more and more in the Lord. I began meditating on His Word, praying more and hearing God clearly for myself.

"Therefore, if any man be in Christ, he is a new creature: old things are passed away; behold, all things are become new"

2 Corinthians 5:17-18

Letting Go

One night, God spoke to me concerning the relationship that I was in. I heard God tell me to separate myself from him. I sat there and cried like a baby because I didn't want to leave. Everything was going so well and at first, I couldn't imagine leaving what I thought was a good thing. But let me tell you one thing about me—when God speaks, I listen. It was one of the hardest things I could do. This man truly loved me and treated me so well.

You know when God tells you to do something, it's always for your good. At that moment, I thought God was being mean, but he had a plan that I didn't know. I didn't leave him right away. Instead, I guess you can say that I tried to manipulate God, as if He wasn't God! I said to myself that if I could get my man to go to church, maybe God would let me stay with him. I tried and tried to make him go, but that never happened. Eventually, I gave up and left the relationship.

During this time, I became more involved in church. I learned more about myself and learned to face my own demons. It didn't feel good either. To me, it felt like the more I got closer to God, the more hell I went through. However, I continued to pray, to fast, and to seek God's face. In doing this, I grew stronger and stronger. I refused to give up. Getting saved and giving my life over to God was the best thing I could have ever done. The many trials I faced did not stop; God just gave me the strength to go through them differently. I still dealt with the pain, unforgiveness and hatred I'd always felt. On top of that, I had car repossessions, was homeless, dealt with kids' father drama, and identity issues.

I'm not here to discourage anybody from getting saved, because it's the best thing ever. I just want to be real about how I felt and what I was going through at that time. However, I learned that it was all for God's glory. I must say, God did not allow me to lose my car or lose my house. That was me. But through all the situations that I put myself in, God turned it around and used it for his glory, all while teaching me how to be a better steward over what He blessed me with.

Letting Go

When I got saved, I no longer felt like I was walking around feeling like the walking dead. I went through a new birthing in my life. We know when delivering a baby, there's some adjustments going on in the body that women endure. There's some crying, screaming, pain and agony. That's the same pain we feel in the spirit in our lives. There will be some crying, screaming, pain and agony. The important thing is not to give up.

Life didn't stop there for me. I had a male friend that I'd known for about six years. We would talk but never on the level of a relationship. We were just cool friends. One day, he called me because he was going through something, so I invited him to the church. He came and a few months down the line, he joined the church. I was happy for him. A while after joining the ministry, he decided to ask me out on a date. We started dating for a while, and then as time went on, we decided to get married. Deep down inside, my heart was far from him. I believe I got in it because it felt like it was the right thing to do at the time, and it was something I always wanted. There were other things in the relationship that I was not happy with as well. No, he did not hit or cheat on me.

Let's just say that just because he was a good friend did not mean he was my soulmate.

We were married for a few months and it was the worst few months of my life. While I was married, I got pregnant again with a baby girl. Before her birth, I tried to commit suicide. I was unhappy with my marriage and pregnancy. No, I did not want to kill my child, but I wanted to end everything. I was going through so much pain. I lost my house, my car, and my dignity. All the so-called friends I thought I had, were nowhere to be found. My family was nowhere around. My church family was not there, except my old church leaders. They let me stay there with my kids for a while, until I decided to go back to New York for two months to get myself together. I thought about staying for the long-term, but I said to myself, *"I've come too far to turn back now"*.

It was New Year's Eve when I came back to North Carolina. I had eighty dollars to my name and nowhere to go. I had called my dad and asked him to pick us up from the bus station. It was just my two kids, at the time, and me. I asked him to drop us off at this cheap, raggedy motel in the area; so, he did. Knowing how raggedy this motel was, as a parent I would not have allowed my child and grandchildren to stay there. I would have said, "No, you're coming to stay with me." But nope, not him. Once we pulled up, I got out to go pay for a room. I asked the man how much it would cost for two nights, and he said $83. I told him that all I had was $75, because I had to feed my kids with the rest. He agreed and said that was fine. Once in the room with my kids, I sat on the bed and wept like a baby, wondering how I got here. At the same time, I was trying not to lose my faith in God. Thinking back now, I thank God for my kids and where I've been. My kids gave me so much strength that day. They didn't fuss or make the situation worse, but they embraced me with their love. The two nights I was there was horrible. It was New Year's Eve going into 2008 the night I checked in. I laid on the bed watching the ball drop on television while my kids slept. I will never forget laying there and hearing the people in the next room becoming intimate. It was a mess. I covered my babies' ears in hopes that they would not wake up asking what that noise was.

The day came when I had to check out. I was sitting on the bed asking God what's next and He put a friend of mine in my spirit to call; so, I did. Good thing she worked right across the street. She came by and I told her what was going on. She allowed me to stay with her for a while. I stayed there for about two months. Yes, I was still married but considering the things I was going through, you might as well say I was alone. While staying there, I started working again. I was saving money and trying to figure out where I should go from here. I remember one day I was at work, and a friend of mine came in and ordered something. As I stood there, she looked at me and chuckled as if something was funny, because my husband at the time, turned my phone line off and she knew about it. Like, what type of man or friend was that? I forced myself to forgive and keep moving forward.

When my time was running short there, I asked a church member if I could stay with her. At first, she said, "no". A few days later, she called me and said, "yes". When I moved in, I asked her what made her change her mind; what made her say yes? Well lo and behold, a person that I thought was a friend from church—not just a friend but a person I looked to as a sister--told her not to open her doors to me and my children. This was the same person who chuckled at me that day. Boy oh boy, church folks can be something else. I was hurt but I kept smiling and kept loving.

Then came peter to him, and said, *"Lord, how oft shall my brother sin against me, and I forgive him? Till seven times? Jesus saith unto him, I say not unto thee, until seven times: but, until seventy times seven"* Matthew 18:21-22 (KJV)

As time went on, things started to get a little better. I was still going to church. I was able to buy myself a car, so things started to look up for the most part. I was now about eight months pregnant and I decided to leave the marriage. Things were not getting any better. All we did was argue and I did not want my kids around that. So, the best thing for me to do was leave. I refused to stay in an unhealthy relationship. It wasn't good for me nor my children, so I did what was best. I know that in the past, all my relationships were unhealthy, but as I got older and wanted more for myself, I had to change my thinking. Believe me, it was not easy. I had to walk around with folks judging my decision, especially church folks. However, no one was in my shoes. No one knew the pain I was going through. I've learned rather you're doing good or bad, people are going to talk about you.

One day in church, the pastor mentioned a shift that God was about to make. He spoke about moving to Georgia. He said some families will go and some will stay. At that time in my life, I was totally ready for a change. I knew I was one of the families leaving but I still prayed about it. Once God spoke to me about this move, I began to get things together. While doing all of this, people thought I was crazy. My mom thought I was losing my mind, but you know when God tells you to do something that others may not understand, it will always look crazy.

I was now the month of June and time for me to give birth to my daughter. It was a bitter-sweet moment. The sweet moment was that she was a healthy baby girl who carried so much love. The bitter moment was that I did not want to be bothered with my ex-husband nor anything that was connected to him. A strong depression came over me. I said to myself, "Here I go again, leaving a relationship like my first relationship, but stuck with his child". However, God gave me the strength I needed to stand. I will tell you the truth though; it was still hard. There I was, with three kids still living with my friend, but I made it work and continued to do what I needed to do for my children in preparation for the move. Before I moved to Georgia, I asked my father if I could stay with him until I was to leave. My daughter was about a month old so I guess that's the reason he said yes. While staying there, I was still working and saving money to move. I must say that staying there showed my dad how strong his daughter really was. He saw firsthand that I didn't give up no matter what came my way. We built a stronger bond in a totally different way. It was a bond of mutual respect.

The time was getting closer and months were counting down when the big move was about to take place. A few weeks before moving I took my two oldest to New York to stay with my mother, and the baby stayed in

Died at Birth

North Carolina with family. I was still trying to figure out how I was going to get down there plus have the help I needed to unload the truck; when one day I received a phone call from one of my brothers. He was asking me when was the last time I spoke with my ex-boyfriend—the one who took such great care of me. I replied, "I don't remember. Why do you ask?" I had no idea that he was standing right next to him. He got on the phone and we started talking about life.

One day, he came by my dad's house and we talked some more. He was so hurt about everything that took place--with me leaving him, getting married and having another baby. But I tell you, this man took my hand and said that he would always be there for me...and he sure was. This man helped me get down to Georgia. He drove the truck and a friend of his drove the cars. He stopped his life just for me. He stood on his word when it came to me. He was such a blessing in my life when I needed help the most.

Letting Go

"I have shown you in every way, by laboring like this, that you must support the weak. And remember the words of the Lord Jesus, that He said, 'It is more blessed to give than to receive".

Acts 20:35

God's Grace

It was August, 2008 when I moved to Georgia. I was nervous and scared as ever. This was new territory for me, but despite the fear that I had, I knew I was supposed to be there. I was all alone--no family, no friends, just me and my children. I was going through a divorce, rejection, guilt and pain. All I could say to myself was that I was a strong woman to have endured all that I have endured without giving up. I knew I had a purpose that I had to fulfill.

Things started coming along slowly. I enrolled the kids in school and started working. I was getting familiar with the area. I even joined a ministry where the Bishop taught me so much wisdom and knowledge. He was not just a powerful man of God, but a man who also loved his people. This ministry was different because I went from a smaller ministry with more of a close family-type atmosphere, to a mega ministry with thousands of members. My

Bishop and the ministry helped me when I needed them the most. When I joined, I was broken in pieces and every time I went to church, he preached a message that was always on time to help me elevate from where I was.

One day, I was sitting on my bed flipping through some papers and I saw an advertisement about school in the medical field. I thought about it, pondered on it, and decided to go down to the school to get more information about the program. Once I got to the back with the counselor, he started talking to me about the program. He said something that messed up the whole idea of me going back to school. It was the hours I had to be in class. I had to be there from 8am to 3pm. I asked myself, "how can I do that and still work?" He offered evening classes but that wasn't going to work either because I had no one to watch my kids.

I ended up telling them that I had to think about it. Weeks went by and I received a phone call from the school asking me to come back in; so, I did. We talked some more but this time with another person. They said the same thing but I told them I could not do it and I left. I went home pondering on how I was going to do this because deep down inside I wanted better; and besides, I wanted to go back to college. The job I was working was not helping. I prayed about it, asking God what I should do but there was no answer. A few more days went by and the school called me again. This time, it was the head director of the school. He was talking to me and I was telling him my reason for not wanting to attend—not because I didn't want to go back to school, but because I was in a hard situation. He asked if I could come in and talk one more time. It took me a minute but I went back down to the school.

I met up with the director and he called me back in his office and started talking to me. This time, I knew it had to be nobody but God that was speaking through this man. I started to cry right there in his office. He encouraged me with the words he spoke and said things that opened my eyes. I decided to do the day classes.

I went back home and I prayed and prayed and asked God to keep me and my family. That night when I went to bed, I had a dream that was so prophetic. At that moment, I knew I was doing what God wanted me to do. The devil was mad at me in that dream because I chose to step out on faith and go back to school. The next day I went to work and gave my manager my two weeks' notice. Classes started on my son's birthday, May 18th. My last day at work was May 15th. I told only my children and a couple of friends. They both thought I was crazy. They asked me how I was going to pay my bills. I started to laugh and say that I didn't know. All I knew was that God told me to go and He would provide all my needs.

The day came when I started class. Mind you, at this point in my life, all I could do was focus on what God told me to do. I did not have time for a relationship, nor anything else. My eyes and ears were on God. This was not the time to get off track. It was not the time to worry about things that were going on around me. All I could do is look up to God. Some may say that I had public assistance to help me with bills and rent. LOL! Not here in Georgia! I sometimes received help with a bill, but not rent. All I had was God.

Five months of me being in school, things were going great. But let me remind you, rent is due each month. My rent was behind for four months, but I was not worried and neither did I ask anyone for help. I thought about asking my mother, but at the time I never told her that I quit my job to go to school. Besides, I took God up on His word because He told me He would supply all my needs and this was a big need.

I would get letters on my door saying I owe and I would ask for a little more time. God granted me favor every time with the leasing office. There were times when I went in there and the lady in the office would have an attitude but God worked things out anyway. The day was coming when I was supposed to receive my student funds, but that was not until the following week. One day, I was coming home and there was another letter on the door; but this letter was different. The total I needed for my rent was $1685.95, but let me tell you how my God works.

Like I said, when I got home there was a bright orange letter on my door. When I opened the letter, the first thing I saw in bold letters was, YOU MUST BE BLESSED. I kept reading and the letter said, *if you can bring in $585, we will erase the remaining balance.* However, it had to be in by that Friday of that week. I went in my house and started shouting and praising God! But wait...that was not it! God had it worked out from the beginning. The lady that worked in the leasing office with the bad attitude got fired. I said to myself, "what happened? What made her change her mind?" There was a man in there who had taken over. Now remember, I said my money wasn't coming until the following week; not the week I needed the rent. Again, God granted me favor until I could pay it. God is so amazing! He worked things out for my good and continued.

Things were looking good and it was now getting close to the holidays. I had purchased gifts for my kids and my mother helped me out as well, so no worries there. I had all I needed for my children for Christmas. One day, a week before Christmas to be exact, I was coming home and saw nothing but devastation. Someone broke into my house and stole all my kids' things, plus more. I felt so violated. I was extremely discouraged that all my hard work had gone down the drain. They went upstairs in my bedrooms; they took food and everything. I was pissed. I called the cops but they did nothing at all. The next day I went back to school and I told my teacher what happened. The class was in shock that I had even come to school that day, but I could not let what happened cause me to miss class. Like fore mentioned, I had to stay focused. People at school helped and gave me gift cards for my family, but I was still hurt and upset. Now you know there's always one person who must make things worse with their comments. There was a lady in my class who thought I was lying about the whole thing. All I could do was look at her and shake my head. Please heed this advice, "In all things, when God speaks, please listen". Prior to this incident, on that Monday I had heard God tell me to take my gifts to a friend's house. Because Christmas was so near, I turned deaf ear to the warning. That Wednesday when came in from school, I found that my home hand been vandalized. God in his infinite wisdom was trying to warn me that this was going to happen. My disobedience gave place to the enemy to transgress against me.

That wasn't it. After the holidays were over and it was the first day back to school for my kids and me, these jokers came back and broke in again! What the heck?!? At that point, I was ready to move. I was done. The good thing is, about three weeks later the cops called me to inform me that they caught the people who broke into my house. The crazy thing is that it was a bunch of teenagers. It was around tax season, so I took my money and used it to move to another city. It was a much better environment for the kids and had better schools. That July, I graduated college and got a new job working in the medical field. Things were coming along a lot better for me.

Now, I'd been living in Georgia for about 2 years and I continued to keep to myself. I was not even in a relationship. It was just me and my little family. From time to time, I would go over to other family member's house who has also moved down here, but other than that, it was work, church and home. I didn't have time for a relationship, so I made a commitment that I was going to be celibate until God blessed me with a husband. I was not trying to look for no man, or just someone to sleep with to help me feel good for the night. It was not always easy. No, no, no! I had to ask God to help me get rid of the feeling of wanting sex. I had to anoint my little sunshine down there and tell it to wait! LOL! Excuse me but this is real talk. This is the part of the book when I must say, LET'S KEEP IT REAL!!!

See, we have too many people out there, both male and female, trying to live right and we as believers don't want to tell the truth and keep it real with these folks. We act like once getting saved, we are all holy. No ma'am, no sir! Not so. When I got saved, no one told me about this part. I had to learn on my own; and the devil didn't make it any better. Let me tell you what he tried to do to me. I would be sleeping and I would have dreams about me having sex. Then I'd wake up hot and bothered. That's not even it. I would be in a store and every cucumber, banana, pickle, etc. started looking like a penis instead of the fruit it was. My eyes were playing tricks on me, but that's how the devil works. He knows your weakness and he will play on that. He would have somebody whisper in my ear what I wanted to hear. But nope! I couldn't go there. I could not even watch current movies with sex scenes because I knew what I was dealing with. I'm telling you, this is real talk and I am not the only person who has dealt with this.

When we are trying to change our ways, we may ask God to take a habit away from us, but we must help ourselves as well. If you know you have an addiction—whether it's weed, crack, alcohol, sex, porn, or whatever--why would you continue to affiliate yourself with the crowd. I lost a lot of friends when I stopped smoking weed, but I expected that.

When you want something different, you must do something different.

Still Standing

It has now been five years since I've been in Georgia and I'm still standing on God's promises. I started working a good job in the medical field, my son was in middle school, and my two girls were in elementary school. I kept my children in different activities. Things were going well. I was even still in ministry. God matured me in so many ways. He helped me to be a better mother as well as a better person. I still had trials that I went through, but I had strength to keep moving.

There were many times when I did not have enough money to pay all my bills. There was even a time when my lights got shut off, but as a mother, I made it work. It was called flashlights and candles. There was also a time when my lights were on, but we had no gas to have hot water. Again, as a mother, I made that work too. I boiled water, poured it in a bathtub with cold water, now you have warm water! It was called survival. It was not because I spent money wrong; sometimes I just did not have enough money for all my bills.

Every time I was down to my lowest, God was always there to pull me back up. There were times when God would allow me to sit in a test to learn from it. I remember the job I was working at for four years—the job I dedicated myself to. This was the same job that when the office was about to shut down, the power of God came over me and I prayed for that business, that God would allow the office to stay open. This was the job that I called my second family, and it was the same job that sabotaged me and let me go. Was I hurt? Oh, yeah! But through all of that, God showed me some things in me that I needed to work on. There was a time God had me go back to that job and pray for the manager who sabotaged me, and I did. Trust me, I did not care to do it, but my heart said something else and obedience followed.

Now let's talk about ministry. Like I mentioned before, I was in a mega ministry, but I started to get bored. It wasn't because my bishop bored me, but because I knew there was more to me than just a seat warmer. I knew God had more for me to do in life and to fulfill my calling. A friend of mine was telling me about this church she visited and wanted me to go, so I went. It was a much smaller church, but I enjoyed it. I loved it, so I joined. I believe God put me there for a season to grow in the calling that He called me to. As I continued to be a part of that ministry, God started to use me in such a mighty way. I started to walk in my calling. I started to be active in the ministry. I met new ladies and drew closer to a few. There were some things I didn't like about the ministry. None the less, my mission was to stay focused on what God had for me to do in that season.

I became close with the pastor and first lady of that house. They pour the things I needed in to me and became my spiritual mentors. I experienced God at whole new level.

What the bishop from the other ministry taught me was equally valuable. As my spiritual father, he poured so much into me, when I was broken. He believed in me when I didn't believe in me. Every time I saw him, my spirit would jump. There will always be a connection. I just believe, each person carries an anointing and gift on them that we need and we must grow in each area God takes us to. No, I'm not saying hop from church to church. But you must hear from God in each area of your life.

God was trying to elevate me in a different way. I had to follow His plan for my life. Bishop had an anointing to love people, to give, and an anointing for wealth. What he poured in me through his teaching is what I needed. So, when God opens doors for me, I would know how to handle it. At the new church, the mantle placed on them was one of deliverance and healing, so I sat and learned the things that I needed to grow. As I got older and more mature in God's Word, I saw a lot and learned a lot. I learned that in ministry, you better know God for yourself because people will steer you wrong if you are not smart and strong enough to know right from wrong. I'm not saying that's what happened here, but just in my years of ministry, I saw a lot and had to learn God for myself, and what He wants for me and my family.

Close to my second year in this ministry, God spoke to me concerning marriage, but it went in one ear and out the other. I'd gotten to the point where I did not want to be bothered with relationships anymore. One day, the lady of the house prophesied that she heard wedding bells. Bishop, had also taught a series on family and relationships during that period.

There was a man who came in the church and joined the church but looking back now, he had the wrong motive. He was just looking for somebody to sleep with. People would say things like, "you two look good together." I would say, "no we don't." You know the enemy works in such a sneaky way, right? All of that "you look good together" stuff started to play in my head. I knew the man liked me but I was so caught up in God I had no time for him. But look how sneaky this devil was; because the devil knew I wasn't going to fall for it if he came straight to me. So, he went to my leader and asked about me and I thought that was the cutest thing. So, we talked, went on a date, and then things started to get deeper. The crazy thing is, before I met this man, I had a dream that I was talking to someone, but in the dream God showed me that he was fake. Nothing about his facade of a genuine guy was true. I got so caught up with the relationship that I forgot about the dream. God will always warn you. That's why it is so important to stay in tune with Him.

One day, we took a picture together and somebody posted it on social media. LOL! Things came out then! I got a message from this lady and you know the rest. So of course, I questioned him but he denied it. He said it was an ex from his hometown. So, we continued until it happened again and I was completely done. Like I mentioned before, I refuse to let a man treat me less than what God called me to be. I would not allow a man to mistreat me, disrespect me or my children another day of my life. I realized who I was and whose I was. It was not worth my self-dignity nor my self-worth. I'm a princess in the eyes of God and the man that God had for me had to see me the same way. I also learned to never allow people to dictate a relationship for you because at the end of the day, when doors close, it's just you and the other person. I don't care how good it may look—looks can be deceiving.

At that point in my life, I told God I wanted to be single. I didn't want to be bothered and I kept to myself. It was going on 2016 and people kept prophesying marriage. I would look at them like they were crazy. It was New Year's Eve and we had a church service. Once again, someone mentioned that word—marriage. It was as if God did not want me to get discouraged or give up on the idea.

I few months prior, I'd asked God a question, "Why couldn't I be with my ex. The one who treated me like a woman was supposed to be treated. God, that relationship was going so well with the except of some minor challenges on his behalf". In the midst, God, He stopped me and challenged, "What did I tell you to do concerning this relationship?"

I replied, "You said separate".

He confirmed, "Yes, I said separate. I never said that was the end of the relationship. I caused you to separate so that I could do a work in you and in him. I heard every prayer that you prayed for him, but it was in my timing, my daughter."

I was complete awed! I told God that if he was supposed to be my husband, then I needed Him to confirm that to me. I didn't want to make any more mistakes. I wanted confirmation from God—not people. Sometimes, people will say things to you that you want to hear, as opposed to the truth. God told me that I will receive a phone call, but God did not say from whom.

New Year's Day, I was coming from the mall with my children. Somewhere between 7 and 8pm, guess who called? My ex-boyfriend! Inside, I was happy. But at the same time, I had a wall up because I just gotten over a relationship. Even though I knew my ex, I still had some concerns. As he started to talk, he was saying things that only God knew. I only talked to God about it. The whole time we were separated, God was working on things in him that I did not know. No longer was he on the streets or drinking. All I can say is that God answers prayers!

As we talked more often, the relationship started to get serious. I continued to keep things to myself. No one in the church knew about him; only my children's Godparents. After a few months, he came down for a visit. I invited him to the church. Boy, oh boy! All I can say is, church folks are so judgmental. I remember someone in the church whispered in my ear and said, "If he ever hits you, let me know." You should have seen my reaction. Just because he's a big guy and didn't have a two-piece suit on did not mean he was dangerous. That's why some people don't come to church now. The minute they walk in the door, they are being judged. A man or woman can look good on the outside, but may be jacked up inside. The scripture says in Romans 2:

1-3, "Therefore you are inexcusable, O man, whoever you are who judge, for in whatever you judge another you condemn yourself; for you who judge practice the same things. But we know that the judgment of God is according to truth against those who practice such things. And do you think this, O man, you who judge those practicing such things, and doing the same, that you will escape the judgment of God?"

When I was dating a man that looked like he had it all together, he turned out to be a mess, and no one said anything to me about that. The moment I brought this guy in the house of God, people had something to say. But I continued to walk in love, despite what I seen and heard.

On April 30, 2016, we got married! It was a small intimate wedding. I said to myself that I couldn't believe that I was finally marrying someone just for me. I couldn't believe that not only did God bless me, but he loved me so much that he gave me the desires of my heart. I am forever grateful! I did not care how people felt. People talked, but I knew he was the one. When God speaks to you about a thing or a person, that's all the confirmation you need. If you trust God, you must also trust His plan. A little before and even after I got married, I started to see a lot. I started to see the people who were truly happy for me, and those who weren't. When I was in the relationship with that other man, I had people all around me. But when things changed, no one was around. Some people can portray like they have your best interest at heart, but the reality is just the opposite.

I married a man who loved me for who I was, who I am, and who I am going to become. He is the man God created just for me. He's not just a dad, but a father. He is a man whom God put his love in- -a caring man. He's a man who may look like he's from the streets, but his heart is made of gold. That's the man I fell in love with. This man doesn't look at my faults. This man stands with me and uplifts me instead of tearing me down. This man helps me push towards the purpose that God has for me. He doesn't care about the stretch marks nor the brokenness that I've been through. Nope! He loves me just how I am—the good, the bad, and the ugly. He satisfies my womanhood and he's a great provider. Oh, yes, yes, yes! That's my man!!! A man I can lay down with and not worry about him cheating on me. A man who is there when the kids need him, and my children adore him. He's a man who is a lover, not a fighter. He's a man who knows how to go out and work hard for his family. Oh, what a mighty man he is! God blessed me with this man not just for me, but to show other women that there's a second chance in love. Don't give up! I went through four bad relationships until God blessed me with him. At the beginning of my story, I said that I couldn't believe this was happening for me because of all the hell I went through, but I'm still standing here to tell my story. Ladies, don't give up! God has you in the palm of his hands.

Words of Encouragement

When I first started to write this book, I had no idea where to begin. I was concerned and worried about how people would look at me, but God brought me through too much to keep my mouth closed. He has given me strength to continue to move forward and share my story. I wanted to share not just for me to get free from my past, but to help someone else get free.

I want to encourage that young lady who thinks it's over...It's **not** over until God says so. If God did it for me, He can do the same for you. At the time that my home was infected with that drug, I thought life was over. At the time that man tried to violate me, I thought life was over. The time I was in a physically and mentally abusive relationship, I thought, *this is it; life is over for me,* but God had a plan. I don't regret what happened in my life, because it made me the woman that I am today—strong, powerful, anointed and beautiful. Yes, I still have things to work on but I'm far from where I used to be. God is so mighty! God's promise in Deuteronomy 31:6 *"Be strong and courageous. Do not be afraid or terrified because of them, for the LORD your God goes with you; he will never leave you nor forsake you."*

We may feel that God is not around. We may feel like God left us, but He is right there. Just when we least expect it, God always shows up. We must count the blessings that God has put right in front of us. Too many times, we get caught up and forget what God has already done for us. No one wants to ever go through pain and suffering but during it all, God can change our situation. When we learn to love ourselves, then others can love us the way we need to be loved.

Words of Encouragement

As you continue to do your part, God will do His. Continue to pray. Continue to hear from God for yourself. Be confident in yourself. Educate yourself. Love yourself. But most of all, learn to love your enemies. As hard as it may be, you must do it. Not for them, but for yourself. Do not allow anyone to have power over you. Try not to walk with a grudge because not letting go causes bitterness, unforgiveness and anger.

Some reading may say, "I forgave that person already." But ask yourself, if you ever see that person again in the streets, would your body vex from all the hurt and pain they put you through? If your answer was yes, then you still have some healing to do. I pray and ask God to deliver you from him/her. If your answer was no, then praise God for healing you! Believe me, it's nothing like letting go and letting God really, deliver you and take that pain away.

I can now say that I have love for every individual who hurt me, stepped on me, talked about me, etc. I learned not to worry about what people say. I am who God says I am. I refuse to allow people to take my peace of mind. I'm in a place in my life where I've never been before. The only way it can be taken from me is if I allow someone to take it. There will still be trials and tribulations that will come up, but you must stand and know God will work things out for your good.

When we put ourselves in situations, it is not God's fault. It is just a lack of obedience on our part. But when we are in that place, that's not the time to walk around mad at the world because of our disappointment. That's the time to give God praise because it could be worse. I used to walk around mad at God as if it was His fault. Yes, there will be times when God may put you in a situation, but it's not to harm you. God wants to see your reaction in the midst of it. Are you going to walk around mad at people who were always there for you? Are you going to walk around mad at God? Are you going to walk around not speaking to folks? No, that's not going to solve anything. Be strong in the Lord and ask God to give you strength.

I'm far from perfect, but I got to a place where I saw life so differently. I truly learned to love people right where they were. I saw that life was too short to hold on to something that I could not change. When I went through all that I went through, from the time I was a child even into adulthood, I could have done three things—walked around depressed and become a drug addict, become very promiscuous, or forgive and get my life right with God. I could be walking around with a grudge towards my parents, but I refuse to because God said to honor thy mother and thy father. Instead of being upset, I loved them in the midst of all the hurt they may have caused me or what they may have done to themselves.

I could walk around hating other people who hurt me but I refuse to give them the power. If I continued to walk around the way I used to be, I would have missed out on my blessing. God has given me chance after chance to get things right and I did. Let me be honest. Just as people hurt me, I also hurt others. Too many of us are checking for the speck in other people's eyes, that we don't recognize the beam in ours.

"And why do you look at the speck in your brother's eye, but do not perceive the plank in your own eye? [42] Or how can you say to your brother, 'Brother, let me remove the speck that is in your eye,' when you yourself do not see the plank that is in your own eye? Hypocrite! First remove the plank from your own eye, and then you will see clearly to remove the speck that is in your brother's eye." Luke 6:41-42

I want to continue to walk in his glory and get all that He has for me. As people in ministry, we come to church, shout, and speak in tongues; but are we truly giving God our all? Are you truly allowing God to take the pain away or are you trying to do it yourself? Are you trying to fight the battle by yourself? If you do, you will lose or hurt yourself trying to fix things on your own.

Words of Encouragement

My prayer for you...

I pray that every individual reading this book will be blessed. I pray that God will continue to cover you. I pray that God will overshadow you with His love and grace. I pray that God will give you strength to keep going. I pray as God healed me, He will do the same for you.

To the young lady who may have been raped and feel violated, just know that God sees all and He will keep you if you want to be kept. I pray the love of Christ will keep your mind and give you the strength you need to move forward.

I pray for the man or woman who is thinking about committing suicide. Don't do it! Don't give up! You have people who love you and are willing to embrace you. Just ask God to show you who they are. I pray against the tricks of the enemy that would have you believe that your life is over. Not true! If you have breath in your body, God can still use you. Look at me. I never thought I would be where I am today. But only by the grace of God, He kept me. I could have died when I took all those pills. My daughter could have had a birth defect...but God! He will change your life only if you let Him.

I pray for the mother or father who may be wondering how you're going to make it and how you're going to take care of your kids. If God did it for me, He can do the same for you. Just know that God will provide all of your needs. God will keep you in perfect peace.

Now, I speak wealth over every reader of this book. I pray that God increases you in good health. I pray that God will direct your path. I pray that God wraps His arms around you and love on you. I pray that you get your identity back in Jesus' name.

God, give them the love that you have given me. Give them the strength and power to sustain hardship. Love on them God, as you have loved on me.

Amen.

Love you all!

About the Author

Toya, originally from New York City, now lives in Atlanta, Georgia. Her education in the medical field prepared her to be a medical assistant and phlebotomist. She also has credentials as an event planner/bridal consultant. Toya, perseveres through challenges.

She's charismatic, energetic and love helping others when she can. She serves as a leader in ministries, as well as in her community feeding the homeless. Toya admits, she could not do all what she does without the support of her family. She has been blessed with three birth children David (20), D'Amani (13) and Nevaeh (8); two stepsons and her loving husband. Toya's mantra is, "Never give up on your dreams. Never allow people to dictate your future. Only you can stop you from reaching the mark."

www.ingramcontent.com/pod-product-compliance
Lightning Source LLC
LaVergne TN
LVHW051510070426
835507LV00022B/3038